# A Cat, a Bat, Your Grandma's Hat

## What Is a Noun?

To Molly, Matt and Andy — three very proper nouns
— B P C

To my mum, who has always been crazy about cats, and my dad, who surprised me by bringing home a kitten when I was 10
— J P

**noun:** A word that names a person, animal, place or thing.

# A Cat, a Bat, Your Grandma's Hat

## What Is a Noun?

by Brian P Cleary

illustrated by Jenya Prosmitsky

LERNER BOOKS · LONDON · NEW YORK · MINNEAPOLIS

Hill
is a
noun.
Mill
is a
noun.

4

# Even Uncle Phil is a noun.

**Gown is a noun.**

**Crown is a noun.**

6

In fact,
our whole
hometown
is a noun.

7

If it's a deck,
a duck
or deer,

If it's a
crystal
chandelier,

If it's a train,
or brain,
or frown,

It's elementary –
it's a noun.

9

NouNS can sometimes
be quite proper,

Like
Brooklyn Bridge,

or

Edward
Hopper,

London,
Levis,
Pekinese –

Proper nouns
name all of these.

11

A jail,
a nail,

a bale of hay,
The pool or park in
Which you play,

A quarter, a porter,
a pencil or pear –

Nouns are seen
everywhere.

A
box,
a lip,

a chocolate chip,

A cup or glass
from which you sip,

14

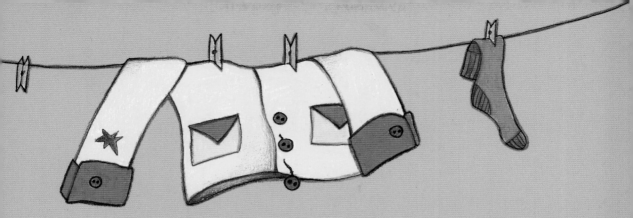

A pocket, button,
sleeve or cuff –

A noun can simply
be your stuff.

A mink,
a drink,
a skating rink,

A cake,
a rake,
your kitchen sink,

16

The pope,
some soap
that's on a rope,
A cold snowman,
a downhill slope.

A
house,
a mouse,
a broken
clock,

WELCOME
TO
SANTA FE

New
Mexico,
an old white
Sock,

Some tar,
a bar,

a baseball star,

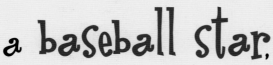

The place where
mother
parks her
car.

RESERVED

19

A noun
can be your
Auntie Lynn,

The **mayor** of the
town you're in,

Your friend
who tells
you corny
jokes —

A noun can be
your favourite folks.

A collar,
a scholar,
a handful
of sand,

Saxes and faxes,
the brass in the band,

A cat, a bat, your grandma's hat —

Nouns are a little of this and that.

23

If it's a place of any kind –

A **mountain**, hall,
or the **windy A9**,

If it's a country,
region or town,

Then surely, shirley,
it's a noun.

And so is a poodle,
cherry strudel,

a fork, a cork,
a curly noodle,

A queen, her nation, a petrol station,

A red raspberry ice machine.

27

If it's a person, place or thing –

Your dad, Dublin, a diamond ring,

LIONS
TIGERS
BEARS

28

If it's a boat or coat or clown,

It's simple, Simon, it's a noun!

# So, what is a noun? Do you know?

## ABOUT THE AUTHOR & ILLUSTRATOR

**BRIAN P CLEARY** is the author of the best-selling Words Are CATegorical™ series and the Math Is CATegorical™ series, as well as <u>Peanut Butter and Jellyfishes: A Very Silly Alphabet Book</u>, <u>Rainbow Soup: Adventures in Poetry</u> and <u>Rhyme & PUNishment: Adventures in Wordplay</u>. Mr Cleary lives in Cleveland, Ohio, USA.

**JENYA PROSMITSKY** grew up and studied art in Kishinev, Moldova. Her two cats, Henry and Freddy, were vital to her illustrations for this book.

Text copyright © 1999 by Lerner Publishing Group, Inc.

First published in the United States of America in 1999

First published in the United Kingdom in 2009 by
Lerner Books,
Dalton House,
60 Windsor Avenue,
London SW19 2RR

Website address: www.lernerbooks.co.uk

This edition was updated and edited for UK publication by Discovery Books Ltd.,
Unit 3, 37 Watling Street, Leintwardine, Shropshire, SY7 0LW


British Library Cataloguing in Publication Data


Cleary, Brian P., 1959–
A cat, a bat, your grandma's hat : what is a noun?. – 2nd ed. –
(Words are categorical)
1. English language – Noun – Juvenile poetry
I. Title
425.5'4


ISBN-13: 978 0 7613 4269 4


Printed in China